D1533099

Published by Larison & Associates
Spokane, WA

Build a Better Business

AUTHOR'S ACKNOWLEDGEMENT

Thanks to all you readers....I hope you find the information and concepts in this book valid, easy to understand and useful in "Building A Better Business" and achieving a process of continuous performance improvement for your business!

Thanks to my editorial assistants, Susan, Alex, Pamela, Tom and Leslie, for helping me compose and structure the book. Their insights and input were invaluable.

Warmest regards,
Hoyt H. (Larry) Larison

"This book is not strictly intended for founding a business but for re-founding any size business. It is profound and almost every line imparts years of accumulated wisdom. As such, it deserves to be reviewed carefully."

-Tom Harpole, award-winning author of fiction and nonfiction, who has worked on assignment for Smithsonian, National Geographic, Outside, and many other literary and trade journals.

ABOUT THE AUTHOR

For thirty-one years, Hoyt H. (Larry) Larison served as President and CEO of Columbia Paint & Coatings Inc., a highly respected and successful manufacturer and distributor of architectural and industrial paints and coatings. The company marketed its products primarily in the Mountain West and Pacific Northwest, including Alaska.

When Columbia Paint & Coatings was sold to a multi-national coatings company, it was for the highest price ever paid for a business of its kind as a multiple of sales, net profit, or of EBITDA (Earnings Before Interest, Tax, Depreciation, Amortization). Columbia Paint was a privately owned company, but never had a majority shareholder or a majority of ownership on the payroll. To assure professionalism in management, Columbia's Board of Directors was elected annually by the Shareholders and its corporate officers were elected annually by its Board of Directors. With this process of Director and Officer selection, the company was operated more like a public company than a private company, and accountability for maintaining profitable growth was a key factor in all Columbia management personnel annual reviews. Columbia Paint & Coatings maintained an aggressive dividend policy and paid 50% of after tax profits to shareholders as dividends.

Under Mr. Larison's leadership, certain management policies and practices evolved that were intended to, and did, create a process of continuous performance improvement that sustained accelerating profitable growth. This evolution of a business philosophy became the foundation of Mr. Larison's Columbia Management System™ program and its Points of Focus and Protocols – which are the basis for this book and its approach to organizational management.

The excellent rate of growth and the ultimate sale of Columbia Paint & Coatings, Inc. can be largely attributed to the management style expressed in the Columbia Management System. Mr. Larison, and his management team at Columbia Paint, developed a thorough understanding of the measures a successful, profitable, company needs to employ in business planning, and in the development of corporate culture and structure. They developed, refined and improved integrated management systems that effectively and efficiently coordinated the inter- and intra- departmental activities of: Sales and Marketing, Information Technology, Accounting and Finance, Credit, Research and Development, Purchasing, Manufacturing, Warehouse and Shipping, Human Resources, Retail/Wholesale Store Development, and Direct Selling efforts.

The approach to operating a business, represented by the Points of Focus and Protocols in Mr. Larison's Columbia Management System program, has also been used to: create detailed business plans; facilitate succession plans; structure compensation and benefit programs; manage litigation; assist with business mergers, acquisitions and sales; and reorganize and restructure existing aspects of business.
Mr. Larison was very active in, and Chairman of, the American Coatings Association, the legislative and regulatory advocacy organization for the United States Paint and Coatings Industry. He served as Director, Chairman, or President for many industry organizations dedicated to business networking and facilitating meaningful information exchange between industry members.
After Columbia Paint was sold, Mr. Larison began formulating a new business model for his consulting practice based on his experiences with Columbia Paint and other for-profit and nonprofit organizations, in conjunction with his continuous performance improvement program's positive effect on their organizational efficiencies and profitability.

The Columbia Management System, based on the Points of Focus and Protocols discussed in the following chapters, will provide tools that every successful company can employ to ensure their business's overall financial strength and market presence. They have been effectively used by many of the organizations Mr. Larison has worked with over the years. They will work to create continuous performance improvement for any organization regardless of its current size, long-range goals or market share position. Some of Mr. Larison's executive roles follow.

FOR-PROFIT ORGANIZATIONS

Columbia Paint & Coatings
President & CEO
A regional paint and coatings manufacturing and distribution company with products and services offered throughout the Mountain West and Pacific Northwest, headquartered in Spokane, WA, during Mr. Larison's term as President & CEO.

American Chemet Corporation
Chicago, Illinois & Helena, Montana
Director & Chairman of the Board
Metal-based chemicals manufacturer
& marketer with international sales

Lyndale Partnerships/LLC's
Managing Partner
Real estate investments and development

Finnaren & Haley, Inc.
Philadelphia, Pennsylvania
Board of Advisors
Architectural & industrial paint and coatings manufacturer

Columbia Real Estate Holdings, LLC
Managing Partner
Real estate investment group
Managing certain properties for Columbia Paint & Coatings shareholders after sale of that company

Shareholder Representative LLC
Managing Partner
Escrowed fund investments and related transactions for Columbia Paint & Coatings shareholders

NOT FOR-PROFIT ORGANIZATIONS

Federal Reserve Bank 12th District
San Francisco, California
Director, Seattle branch
Federal Reserve Bank System USA

American Coatings Association
Director, Vice Chairman of the Board, and Vice Chairman
Architectural Coatings Committee
Primary legislative and regulatory advisory association for
US Paint & Coatings industry

National Federation of Independent Business
Director and Trustee
Board of Advisors
Largest legislative and regulatory advocacy business organization
in the United States with over 400,000 members

Color Guild Incorporated
President, Vice President, Board of Directors
International association of paint manufacturing firms for the
development of color marketing programs

Northwest Paint Council
Chairman
A regulatory and legislative advocacy group specific to Washington
and Oregon for the American Coatings Association

Guild CPO International
President, Vice President, and Board of Directors
An international raw material and container buying cooperative
for regional paint manufacturers

Spokane Country Club
President, Chairman: golf course Master-Plan Committee, Member

White House Conference on Small Business
Presidential Appointee

Young Presidents Organization
Member
International organization of corporate executives who became
President of their organization prior to the age of 39

Republican National Committee
Small Business Advisory Council
Chairman
Developed small business platform positions for President Ronald Reagan's
second term

Whitworth University
Spokane, Washington
Business School Advisory Board Member

Mobius Science Center
Spokane, Washington
Member, Board of Directors

Spokane County Boys and Girls Clubs
Spokane, Washington
Member, Board of Directors

TESTIMONIALS

"Columbia Paint and Coatings was one of the most dynamic, successful and best managed companies I have had the pleasure to work with. Larry Larison did a great job of growing value for the Columbia shareholders."

> *-D. Michael Jones, Former President & CEO of Banner Bank*
> *and Former Director of Columbia Paint & Coatings*

"Larry put together a great management team and management system that led Columbia Paint & Coatings to become one of the leading coatings companies in the US and also one of the most profitable. His management style emphasized teamwork, goal setting and planning including follow-up and rewarding goal achievement with recognition and profit based bonus compensation...and it really worked well."

> *-Eric Schindler*
> *Former CFO of Blue Cross Blue Shield of Montana*
> *Former CFO of Columbia Paint & Coatings*

"Larry Larison has been an invaluable member of American Chemet's Board of Directors and an excellent Chairman of the Board for Chemet. Larry's management philosophy and participation in our Executive Staff functions have helped American Chemet to achieve its current position as a leading and very profitable producer of zinc and copper metals with distribution worldwide."

> *-W.W. Shropshire Jr.*
> *Chairman of the Board of Directors of American*
> *Chemet Corporation*
> *Former Director Columbia Paint & Coatings*

"Larry Larison did a great job for the shareholders of Columbia Paint and Coatings. Larry's leadership produced accelerating profitable growth, which led to a very successful sale of the business! One of the best and most organized companies I have ever worked with!"

-Thomas Osborne
Former CEO of the Tnemec Company
Former CEO of the Glidden Company and ICI
Paints North America
Former Director Columbia Paint & Coatings

Table of Contents

Foreword 12

CHAPTER ONE: POINTS OF FOCUS 17-39

Introduction to Points of Focus 18

10 Points of Focus 18

- Point of Focus 1
  *Maintain a passionate commitment to profitably grow the business while
  maintaining a strong balance sheet* 20

- Point of Focus 2
  *Treat all individuals and organizations you deal with in a fair, honest and
  ethical manner* 22

- Point of Focus 3
  *Recognize that each employee is a team member and maintain a strong
  commitment to team building and team member education* 24

- Point of Focus 4
  *Identify the "vital few" areas of focus for the organization that represent the
  greatest opportunity for profit improvement* 26

- Point of Focus 5
  Get the "right person" in every position. Make changes when called for 28

- Point of Focus 6
  *Maintain and continuously improve your product offering so that you are the
  supplier of choice for an expanding customer base* 30

- Point of Focus 7
  *Implement a thorough, accurate reporting and performance-to-goals
  review system* 32

- Point of Focus 8
  *Maintain a commitment to develop products, programs and initiatives that
  are designed to maintain and enhance a healthy environment in all the
  communities and countries in which you operate* 34

- Point of Focus 9
  *Maintain a commitment to comply with all laws and regulations in all the
  communities and countries in which you operate* 36

- Point of Focus 10
  *Strive to be a good corporate citizen in all the communities and countries you
  do business in by participating in activities and organizations that are
  engaged in helping the environment, ecology and economy, achieve and
  maintain a process of continuous improvement* 38

CHAPTER TWO: PROTOCOLS **41-90**

Introduction to Protocols 42

10 Protocols 43

- Protocol 1
  Organizational Structure 44

- Protocol 2
  Goal Setting and Planning 48

- Protocol 3
  Product Development 52

- Protocol 4
  Communications 58

- Protocol 5
  Customer-Driven Market Analysis/Market Strategy 64

- Protocol 6
  Profit and/or Goal Achievement-Driven Incentives 70

- Protocol 7
  Team Member (Employee) Job Description & Performance Evaluation 74

- Protocol 8
  Accountability: Monitoring Goals Related Performance 80

- Protocol 9
  Strategic Alliances 84

- Protocol 10
  Team Building 88

Author's Closing Statement 92

Citations: Quotes 94

FOREWORD

The Columbia Management System™ Points of Focus and Protocols discussed in this book represent a business philosophy that was developed from my experience working with various corporate for-profit and not-for-profit organizations. I articulated this philosophy into its current form when I began establishing my consulting practice. I reflected on the evolution of policies and procedures that helped shape Columbia Paint & Coatings, and other organizations I had worked with, into highly successful entities committed to operating with a process of continuous performance improvement.

The Points of Focus and Protocols contained in this guide to business:

- Offer a company-wide strategy that empowers employees at all levels to create a corporate atmosphere of shared goals, a means to reach those goals, and a rewards system based on goal achievement metrics.

- Reinforce the basic mission statement of a company and enable the completion of that mission.

The following is an example of a mission statement. It was developed for Columbia Paint & Coatings during our management team discussions and was refined through feedback from our employees.

Columbia Paint & Coatings Mission Statement

Our Mission is to:

Be the supplier of choice, and the largest market share holder in the markets we serve, by providing excellence in service and product quality for customers that purchase paints, coatings and related surface preparation, application equipment, and materials.

Be an employer that provides a work environment which offers excellent benefits, training and educational programs, in a safe, comfortable workplace and encourages innovation by allowing

*employees the freedom to act, to provide creative solutions,
and to make calculated strategic decisions to reach specific
goals. These are established through a process that includes
input from all employees.*

*Conduct all aspects of our business in a fair, honest
and ethical manner.*

Mission statements in general are usually brief and direct. The policies and strategies which support them are sophisticated and multi-layered, encompassing all aspects of the business.

OVERVIEW OF THE CONCEPTS OF POINTS OF FOCUS AND PROTOCOLS

Points of Focus and Protocols are not new in basic concept to the global business community. They are diligently followed by many successful organizations around the world and they have been present in one form or another since complex, multi-layered business first began. They are principles of success which are not dated by the passing of time. They remain as relevant today as when they were first implemented and remain open to evolve as circumstances dictate.

However, the practices discussed in Points of Focus and Protocols can sometimes be overlooked as integral to an organization's planning, policies and structure during any phase of the business. It is the consistent application of these Points of Focus and Protocols that set an organization apart from its competitors and help define it as a successful, evolving, dynamic entity capable of achieving and maintaining a corporate culture of continuous performance improvement.

Points of Focus and Protocols are not completely separate processes. They are closely related and can be integrated in actual day-to-day business applications. The key to a successful business strategy is in understanding their role in developing, refining and implementing policies, procedures and practices, which empower the business to grow profitably and achieve its goals and accomplish its mission.

Underlying the Points of Focus and Protocols being discussed in this book is a company-wide philosophy that stresses the importance of recognizing internal and external customers in all aspects of a company's business.

INTERNAL CUSTOMER AND EXTERNAL CUSTOMER: *A POWERFUL VIEWPOINT*

Perception in business is a powerful tool, not only in selling products and providing services but also in how a company is viewed internally by its employees and externally by those with whom it conducts business. Learning to view fellow employees as customers within the departments of your company strengthens interpersonal relationships within the company setting. The concept is simple in execution but powerful in impact.

Internal customers are employees: anyone who is in your employ in a company role is your internal customer, and for them, the power of qualified praise cannot be overstated.

External customers are all other people: anyone who interfaces with your company as a component of doing business. Both groups are stakeholders with an absolute interest in the success of the business.

External customers can be further defined in two ways:

1. The current customer actively purchasing your goods and/or services and providing cash flow and profits to sustain the business. Retaining these customers and expanding your customer base is of the highest priority.

2. External customers are also industry associations with common interests, suppliers of key goods and services to your company such as banks, insurance companies, raw material suppliers, government agencies, etc., whose activities impact your business and the countries and communities in which you conduct business.

IN SUMMARY

In this book, Points of Focus and Protocols are discussed in separate chapters with each Point or Protocol followed by a Why/How discussion. While a certain level of business acumen is assumed for the readership of this book, it is recognized that every business will be at varying stages of development, and the Why/How discussions are meant as baselines from which you can adapt the Points of Focus and Protocols to your own specific business enterprise and/or situation.

Identifying the Points of Focus and understanding the Protocols is the first step in ensuring your company commits to operating with a standard of continuous performance improvement in all aspects of the business. Using these Points and Protocols, and reviewing the Why/How discussions against your own existing policies and procedures, will help you continuously evaluate which areas of your company may need improvement through revitalization or revision to keep it evolving, dynamic and successful, in a constantly changing, challenging and very competitive business environment.

I have seen how effective these Points of Focus and Protocols are when applied consistently in all types and sizes of organizations. By keeping this guide to business condensed to only critical components, I hope that it will become a useful reference for your business.

-Hoyt H. (Larry) Larison

"A Mission Statement is not something you write overnight...But fundamentally, your mission statement becomes your constitution, the solid expression of your vision and values. It becomes the criterion by which you measure everything else."

-Stephen Covey

Chapter One

POINTS OF FOCUS

INTRODUCTION

Points of Focus represent the basic principles of a business philosophy that mirror and support the company's mission statement. Committing to these Points of Focus strengthens the operating standards that your company employs in its internal structure.

INTERNAL AND EXTERNAL CUSTOMER

Each Point of Focus being discussed also recommends that a company recognize and implement a culture which emphasizes the importance of internal and external customer relationships. As discussed in the Foreword, these relationships are critical to ongoing success within the business and within the communities served.

SUMMARY

Points of Focus are principles. Protocols are specific actions. Points of Focus are the reason Protocols are developed and implemented within an organization. Points of Focus are also strategic elements of an overall business philosophy that are geared to ensuring a company's ability to achieve success in the present as well as in the future.

10 POINTS OF FOCUS

Ten Points of Focus develop a culture of continuous performance improvement, which strengthen your mission statement.

1. Maintain a passionate commitment to profitably grow the business while maintaining a strong balance sheet.

2. Treat all individuals and organizations you deal with in a fair, honest and ethical manner.

3. Recognize that each employee is a team member and maintain a strong commitment to team building and team member education.

4. Identify the "vital few" areas of focus for the organization that represent the greatest opportunity for profit improvement.

5. Get the "right person" in every position. Leverage each team member's strengths. Make changes when called for.

6. Maintain and continuously improve your product offering so that you are the supplier of choice for an expanding customer base.

7. Implement a thorough, accurate reporting and performance-to-goals review system.

8. Maintain a commitment to develop products, programs and initiatives that are designed to maintain and enhance a healthy environment in all the communities and countries in which you operate.

9. Maintain a commitment to comply with all laws and regulations in all the communities and countries in which you operate.

10. Strive to be a good corporate citizen in all the communities and countries you do business in by participating in activities and organizations that are engaged in helping the environment, ecology and economy, achieve and maintain a process of continuous performance improvement.

On the following pages, the Points of Focus are examined to determine why they are so vital and how they are applied in the business structure.

Point of Focus 1

Maintain a passionate commitment to profitably grow the business while maintaining a strong balance sheet.

WHY

Profitable growth is a primary goal. Financial strength is required for achieving that goal. One of the foundations of any business is its available cash – cash equates to the immediate accessible financial strength that allows a company to weather an ever-changing business climate.

Business owners are often anxious to achieve growth, and as a consequence, do not regularly review the total implications of the cost of operations and the resulting impact on cash flow and the balance sheet. Managers frequently grow the business faster than its ability to financially sustain itself, and spend more dollars than the company is taking in within a given time frame. This can be true of the most seasoned business executives, who ultimately may have to answer not only to senior management but sometimes to Boards of Directors and Shareholders.

There are key balance sheet ratios that need to be kept in mind at all times so that the company does not run out of cash. These key balance sheet ratios measure the financial flexibility and strength of the company. It is not necessary to go into an in-depth discussion of all balance sheet ratios here as your corporate financial officer, banker, and accounting advisors can review them with you. But in summary, they are the working capital, current ratio and quick ratio. These key balance sheet ratios need to be kept in mind at all times so that the company does not run out of accessible cash. Key balance sheet ratios measure the financial flexibility and strength of the company and, managed properly, allow you to profitably grow the business while maintaining your balance sheet strength.

HOW

There are several ways to manage this key point of focus.
A few suggestions:

- Keep your focus on financially balanced growth and not on growth for growth's sake.

- Key balance sheet ratio budget and guidelines should be established and agreed on by management and regularly evaluated and adjusted throughout the course of the current business year to optimize the organization's financial performance.

- Manage key balance sheet ratios to stay within a generally accepted range or a range established specifically for your business. Consult with your Chief Financial Officer, banker, and accounting professionals at least annually to set the budget ratios needed for optimum performance.

- Make sure you are generating enough cash-on-hand to fund the components of the business that support growth, such as research and development, new store or new market development, new manufacturing, warehousing, etc.

- Constantly strive to improve profitability through strategic pricing and focusing on the sale of products that offer the greatest profit potential.

Point of Focus 2

Treat all individuals and organizations you deal with in a fair, honest and ethical manner.

WHY

In today's developing global economy, it is clearly recognized that a company's ability to deal with others honestly, ethically and consistently is critical to its longevity and its success.

In the current business environment it is necessary to treat people and organizations fairly and ethically. However, perceptions by the public and the press are often that business fails in this effort. The reputation of any business is a vital key to its ability to sustain profitable growth.

Regardless of the stage of your business development, treating others fairly and ethically in all aspects of business is crucial to developing a positive corporate identity, with your employees, and within the communities and countries that you serve. It will enhance your relationships internally with employees, foster communications between departments, and improve relations with customers and suppliers. It will improve your standing in the community and make it easier to negotiate issues vital to your organizational needs.

The reputation developed for treating everyone in an equitable, respectful and consistent manner will empower the sustained professional business relationships that foster growth and support ongoing business success.

HOW

Maintaining consistent policies throughout your company is a key to the success of this Point of Focus. Professional relationships in a dynatmic environment are complex, but this Point of Focus does not have to be so.

- Make this Point of Focus part of discussions related to your mission statement.

- Make this part of ongoing employee training.

- When conducting customer and employee satisfaction surveys, ask if the organization is doing a good job complying with this Point of Focus commitment and make improvements when feedback indicates it is necessary.

- When scheduling internal company meetings, attach a copy of the company's mission statement to the meeting announcement as a means of keeping it front and center of discussions surrounding company performance in this category.

- Encourage innovation: acknowledge the value of risk taking, and the value of rewarding and praising stand-out employees.

Point of Focus 3

Recognize that each employee is a team member and maintain a strong commitment to team building and team member education.

WHY

A winning, intuitive team translates into a successful, dynamic, continually improving company.

All too often in corporations, large or small, management is driven by profit and loss and/or reporting to the board of directors or stockholders. As a result, they may lose sight of the human side of business and how it impacts the bottom line. Every employee, regardless of position, should feel valued by the company. Allowing employees to have a voice in the company, in job-appropriate ways, helps employees feel engaged and empowered. This involvement encourages employees to participate actively in achieving the company's goals and to feel an important part of its successes.

HOW

- Implement a clear, concise and consistent set of policies that are devoted to actively engaging and recognizing employees and to giving them a "voice" or means of participation.

- Recognize that there are two types of customers in business: internal and external. The success of a business depends on meeting the needs of both entities.

- Foster a corporate culture of respect for others: inside the workplace and outside the workplace.

- Follow protocols, such as the ones provided in this book that support and nurture a team environment which values compassion, dignity and qualified praise for positive, determined efforts.

Point of Focus 4

Identify the "vital few" areas of focus for the organization that represent the greatest opportunity for profit improvement.

WHY

With the vital few areas of focus for the corporation identified, they drive the company forward in its quest for continuous performance improvement.

The vital few areas of focus for any corporation are those areas that represent its foundation for generating profitable revenue. These can be products or services and include the markets for those products and/or services. There is a general rule in business that 20% of the products and/or customers will bring in approximately 80% of the company's profitable revenue. While these top tier entities can and do deserve the majority of attention, it is also important to implement and act with due diligence on the remaining customer/product segments that provide supporting cash flow to the company.

Continuous performance improvement policies impact all areas; not just those which are most obvious. During difficult times or periods of expansion, a well-developed, well-planned and effectively marketed product line with major focus on the vital few can provide a foundation of strength. This can include strategic pricing opportunities that allow the company to anticipate and weather negative market fluctuations, competitive pressure, and changing consumer preferences.

HOW

The vital few areas of focus are often identified during the development of the company mission statement. Goals cannot be met unless certain criteria are achieved. Identifying the vital few areas that will provide the company its greatest profit improvement is a first step to employing other Points of Focus which enable the company to then meet performance criteria to achieve its goals.

- Begin by identifying your company's vital few areas of product and consumer segment focus that have the most impact on profit.

- Review these vital few areas of focus at least annually and find ways to improve them.

  Have a clear 5-year corporate business plan in place so that you know how to measure company performance to goals, including the vital few areas for profit-related improvements.

- Gather as much factual information as possible when assessing the vital few areas that give your company its greatest profit potential. Consider the activities of your competition, their market share, their logistics, and their directions as they impact your company market share goals. Then, review this information against the vital few areas you have identified as impactful to profit potential and implement complementary strategies and tactics to outdistance the competition and meet the goals set by your business plan.

Point of Focus 5

Get the" right person" in every position. Leverage each team member's strengths. Make changes when called for.

WHY

Tolerating employee performance below reasonable expectations may eventually foster a corporate culture that accepts and expects mediocre performance, thereby creating an environment which can cause the company to fall behind its competition.

Products and services do not sell themselves – it takes the human factor. Business is a mix of professional and interpersonal dynamics. There is often a tendency, once a business is established, to lapse into a "comfort level" with a particular way of doing business. Sometimes, an employee is promoted on the basis of familiarity or seniority over actual skill sets. In this instance, it is unfair to the employee and the company not to evaluate the transition, and if necessary, provide assistance through new or enhanced skill sets training, during the early stages in the new position.

Anyone who has been with a company for a long time has vested much of himself or herself in the company. One of the most difficult decisions any manager will need to face is to promote, not promote, demote, or terminate an employee. Implementing internal policies and procedures for all management and for all employees in these circumstances that are consistent and clearly delineated, helps make difficult situations less stressful as they are standardized. Remedies include such actions as developing programs for mentoring and training, reassignment criteria, and termination support programs.

The key to this Point of Focus is to make a company commitment to address the subject of employee positions and performance expectations, in a standardized manner, and to put systems into place that address situations that need remedial action.

HOW

Developing the "right person" in every position is a blend of corporate and interpersonal responsibility. Respect for the employee includes the company providing all the tools that the person needs to succeed and grow in each position. The more clearly stated each position in the company, the more standardized its criteria for performance evaluation is the better the company is able to achieve this point of focus.

- Develop a broad, comprehensive employee hiring, training and promoting policy.

- Develop a corporate culture of mentoring. Reward mentors.

- Develop clear and concise job descriptions, skill sets required, and benchmarks for performance.

- Develop a corporate culture that has the strength and commitment to its employees to provide training and avenues for improvement as well as the fortitude to take action when corrective action, including termination, is needed.

Point of Focus 6

Maintain and continuously improve your product offering so that you are the supplier of choice for an expanding customer base.

WHY

Companies in the developed world face competition from exponentially accelerating technology and must improve their product and service offerings accordingly.

It is necessary for all managers and executives to review all aspects of products offered for performance improvement opportunities: development, delivery, expansion, customer service, quality, quantity, etc. Even companies with a long history of successful products, with decades of top tier market share, can find themselves in a position where they are challenged by a new product or a redesigned product.

Nothing is guaranteed. The only way to stay at the forefront is to continually review what you offer and identify new products you can develop to support and strengthen your product lines.

HOW

- Construct product development policies and procedures that empower your sales force to sell to meet changing market conditions.

- Empower your research and development departments to interface directly with sales and marketing departments so that the need for new products can be identified and existing products can be continually improved to meet changing market dynamics.

- Empower your manufacturing department to revise, evaluate and suggest new means of product production so that quality and consistency are continually evolving and improving to the highest possible standards.

- Subscribe to specific trade journals. Look for the cutting edge trends from business sectors that impact or mirror components of your business.

- Keep communications open for all employees so that suggestions can be made to improve product offerings at all levels of the company – you never know where the next great idea will come from. You want to keep that door open for any and all suggestions and possibilities.

Point of Focus 7

Implement a thorough, accurate reporting and performance-to-goals review system.

WHY

Adopting a diligent follow-up system is vital to goals achievement. Each organization needs to commit to continual follow-up policies and to protocols to ensure actual performance is on track to meet or exceed established goals.

Once goals are established, there needs to be a concise system to disseminate information so everyone knows who is responsible for areas of goal achievement and how their progress will be measured in reaching those goals. The more organized, concise and clear your system is, the more frequently the goals are evaluated, the more opportunity there will be for achieving success and for promoting or recognizing the efforts of those who were instrumental in reaching company performance goals.

HOW

There are many options and ways to implement reporting and performance-to-goals review systems. The underlying concept to all successful systems is consistency. Nothing is more confusing to an employee or a department than mixed messages and ever-changing responsibilities that are not clearly delineated against performance criteria.

Point of Focus 7 also encompasses the evaluation and recognition of changing market conditions and identifies where market serving departments need to be enhanced with support, or changed in direction.

- Be consistent in performance criteria needed to evaluate each goal on an annual basis.

- Be consistent in articulating performance criteria for each goal and its related strategies and tactics.

- Be thorough in assessing performance-to-goals against current and changing market conditions.

- Ask for performance input from internal and external customers. Constantly evaluate how social media can best be utilized.

Point of Focus 8

Maintain a commitment to develop products, programs and initiatives that are designed to maintain and enhance a healthy environment in all the communities and countries in which you operate.

WHY

The world has become a global economic and ecological community, and with this transition has come the need for business to commit to a greater role in environmental stewardship.

The public everywhere are concerned for the state of the environment and for their local economies. Appropriate policies and procedures that drive profit for a company are not mutually exclusive to recognizing the needs of local and global communities to have their environment and economies protected and respected.

Recognize that without a healthy environment, there cannot be a healthy economy.

HOW

An ongoing alliance with the regulatory bodies in communities as well as company outreach policies and involvement with environmentally-concerned citizen programs will help the company maintain a positive presence in all markets it serves.

- Maintain a strong corporate presence in the community by joining organizations that support the community's goals related to the maintenance and improvement of the environment.

- Maintain an active and ongoing public relations presence that highlights the company's commitment to the environment and to its public responsibility.

- Address any issues or misunderstandings with a sense of immediacy and urgency to build and maintain trust with local communities relative to environmental issues.

- Maintain active and ongoing safety and monitoring evaluations and security measures in any process that has an environmental risk.

- Address any incidents or accidents in a time-appropriate and corrective manner.

- Maintain a level of transparency as much as is possible to build community trust.

- When developing products or services, be aware of their potential impact in utilization, manufacturing and distribution, and be aware of legislation and regulatory changes that may be enacted in the future.

- Review corporate policies and procedures related to environmental impact on local and regional economies annually and implement changes to optimize desired results.

Point of Focus 9

Maintain a commitment to comply with all laws and regulations in all the communities and countries in which you operate.

WHY

The number of laws and regulations that companies must comply with in order to do business on a global basis is becoming ever more complex and challenging. Compliance is not an issue of a "nice to have" but is a "need to have" in order to stay competitive, on the leading edge of innovation, and to continue accelerating profitable growth.

Globally, legislation and regulation continue to proliferate in terms of their impact on business. Businesses need to be in compliance with increasing local, regional, national, and international laws. When corporations operate in several states or in several countries, managing all the differing laws and requirements can be a challenge. However, as difficult as it is, the challenge must be met in order for the company to continuously improve its performance in competitive markets.

HOW

Develop relationships with political organizations, legislators, community leaders and stay abreast of what is happening in the regions and countries in which you do business. Formulate company policies and procedures for managing all the data which must be collected relative to regulations and have this data readily available to management at all times.

- Keep informed and current on all regulations, laws, and legislation in all communities you serve.

- Maintain a corporate relationship with legislative bodies and regulatory organizations through committee involvement, and community participation via organizations that support these regulatory bodies and the communities.

- Maintain standards of achievable quality controls in all aspects of manufacturing and distribution.

- Maintain evaluation of compliant manufacturing processes on a quarterly basis.

- Develop communication lines for suggestions by employees for any improvements to manufacturing processes that could improve performance related to regulatory compliance.

- Develop and continually improve safety programs, policies, and record systems.

- Develop emergency policies and procedures for unexpected occurrences where environmental risks may occur and develop methodologies for treatment of those risks.

- Include a public relations function in your company structure that is specific to regulation compliance and community relationships.

- Invite inspections and constantly review what is in the safety pipeline. If relevant, conduct public agency recommended emergency drills; OSHA, fire marshals, etc.

Point of Focus 10

Strive to be a good corporate citizen in all the communities you do business in by participating in activities and organizations that are engaged in helping the environment, ecology and economy, achieve and maintain a process of continuous performance improvement.

WHY

Building relationships with other businesses and individuals that are like-minded in the community will strengthen community ties, build trust, and reinforce the principles of your business mission statement.

Joining organizations which provide volunteer opportunities can help your company give back to the community while at the same time developing its reputation, potential business contacts, and perception as a fair and equitable entity. By achieving an active presence in such community activities, the company gains a reputation for helping the community outside of the products and services it offers for profit. It is a dedication of time and service that reflects positively on the company as a whole.

HOW

Identify, within the communities you serve, organizations which are reflective of your own company directions, products, services and values and volunteer or interact with the community through these organizations.

- Get involved. Make it a part of your corporate planning to support the community through work with nonprofits, professional associations, and community drives.

- Allow employees to participate in these efforts by providing several corporate sponsored choices.

- Reinforce internally how representatives of your company will conduct themselves when in service to the community through non-profit efforts, professional associations, or community-driven events.

- Encourage employees to join professional associations and provide a stipend for dues.

- Recognize that each employee who is engaged in community service activities is a public relations opportunity.

- Provide procedures and policies whereby employees who regularly participate in community-driven activities can also communicate feedback received, where company presence in the community could be improved. It is also possible that employees in these settings will receive feedback or comments on products or services the company provides and the feedback can be invaluable to product modifications or product development. Be sure to provide a mechanism for employees to record and communicate this information to management.

Chapter Two

PROTOCOLS

INTRODUCTION

Protocols are actions taken which implement policies and procedures within the company to support the mission statement, facilitate corporate and departmental goal achievement, and foster a culture of continuous performance improvement.

Protocols are also elements of a business philosophy that function to keep your business dynamic and successful in a constantly changing, competitive marketplace. The Protocols recommended in this book can be employed by organizations to achieve exceptional results in maintaining accelerating profitable growth.

While some Protocols may already be in place within your organization, any and all should be evaluated periodically for their overall effectiveness. The success of their implementation correlates to ongoing evaluation of their effectiveness and their ability to modify and adapt to changing business directions.

INTERNAL CUSTOMER AND EXTERNAL CUSTOMER

Internal and external customer concepts are critical to a company's success because they help to maintain balance and stability for your company.

The concepts of internal and external customer, as discussed in the Foreword, are inferred to be a significant underlying principle in the application of Protocols identified in the following pages.

SUMMARY

The following Protocols are guidelines based on the author's experience in working with diverse corporate structures. They are tools that provide a foundation for healthy company growth, while maintaining balanced financial strength. Protocols are a baseline that can be customized and expanded to meet the needs of your organization.

The key to their success is the commitment to consistently evaluate each Protocol for its efficiency and effectiveness in meeting company goals, and to continuously find ways of improving each facet of each Protocol to keep your company operating in all departments to its maximum ability.

"If an organization diligently follows the Points of Focus and Protocols as the basis for its operating policies and procedures, its chances for success will be greatly enhanced and it will surely be able to sustain a corporate culture of continuous performance improvement."

-Hoyt [Larry] Larison

10 PROTOCOLS

Ten Protocols strengthen your mission statement by providing strategic, consistent actions that support a culture of continuous performance improvement.

1. Organizational Structure

2. Goal Setting and Planning

3. Product Development

4. Communications

5. Market Analysis/Market Strategy

6. Profit and/or Goal Achievement-Driven Incentives

7. Team Member (Employee) Job Description and Performance Evaluation

8. Accountability: Monitoring Goals-Related Performance

9. Strategic Alliances

10. Team Building

Protocol 1

Organizational Structure

WHY

Balanced, defined, and refined, structure is important to function effectively in any organization.

The organization chart identifies major areas of function (departments), links job titles with areas of responsibility, and provides the basis for developing accountability systems. Although sometimes its impact on corporate performance can be underestimated, it serves as the foundation of corporate accountability as well as the baseline for establishing performance criteria.

Developing clearly defined organizational structure will assist in keeping the company focused on advancing its mission statement. Defining the corporate structure so that it is clear to all employees as well as management, and refining the structure over time as needed, will stimulate growth, change and keep the company operating smoothly.

Business is a dynamic environment: simultaneously proactive and reactive, defined and refined, stabilizing and growing. Just like the framework of a building that is structurally sound, organizational structure still needs assessment, tweaking, strengthening, and at times, revision.

"A thorough understanding of an organization's structure is essential to those with the responsibility for managing even the smallest component of the operation."

-T. Osborne, Former CEO, the Glidden Company

HOW

- **Define your company's structure simultaneous to developing its mission statement.**

  When forming a business, even though it may initially be with only a small number of employees, identify the major departments, their numbers of employees and their interface. Define responsibilities within each department and between departments. Include in this structural overview, specific guidelines for how each department will interface with internal customers, such as other departments, and with external customers such as suppliers, consumers, and the community. Then identify how you will project their growth and the addition of any other departments so you have a flexible model going forward.

  The best policy is to prepare an organizational chart prior to the startup of any business acknowledging that what seems to work on paper will more than likely need modification as the business begins to establish itself and grow.

- **Periodically, revisit your original organizational structure and modify as needed.**

  Organizational charts may be re-evaluated even if the business is already established. For example, when markets shift, there can be a need to alter company directions and internal responsibilities should adjust accordingly; or, if and when a decision is made to prepare the business for sale, all departments and the levels of responsibility of all jobs currently existing will need to be evaluated to ensure maximum performance and to meet a desired or projected sales price point. Additionally, periodically there will be a need to evaluate and refine the organizational structure so that any areas that are crossover or weak in accountability can be corrected to achieve maximum performance.

- **Develop a professional support system that can assist in reviews of organizational structure at any given stage of business development.**
  Seek advice from executive management and/or any board of directors that is vested in the company, as to organizational structure strengths and weaknesses throughout the life of the company. Evaluation by others can often reveal potential beneficial adaptations to the organization's internal structure.

- **Understand that while an organizational chart is invaluable for defining structure, it is only a guideline, or a foundation, on which to build the business.**
  The organizational chart provides defining structure for the business - but it does not define the business. Entrepreneurs have a certain idea of how they want the business to grow and of the long term goals they wish to achieve. Gut instinct, in conjunction with organized plans and processes, still guide most businesses to success.

- **Keep the organizational chart readily available for access by employees.**
  An organizational chart is a valuable tool to keep accessible to employees. It provides each employee with an overview of the responsibilities and potential lateral and vertical alignment within the company. It can provide each employee with a basis for developing a goal for advancement as well as reinforce the interconnected relationships within the corporation as a whole.

Organizational charts can be kept with each departmental policy and procedural manual as well as with each human resources manual delineating positions, responsibilities and skills sets for all positions.

Management Action Statement:
Organizational Structure

*"Corporate and departmental organization charts were developed
that clearly articulated and defined areas of responsibility
for all key management positions. As the company grew,
and management positions were added, the corporate and
departmental charts were periodically updated and circulated to
all personnel and the board of directors."*

-Hoyt H. [Larry] Larison

Protocol 2

Goal Setting and Planning

WHY

A strategic planning and goal setting system is necessary to define achievable goals, evaluate progress, and to keep a business focused on sustainable growth.

A strategic planning and goal setting system should be established to create meeting systems and protocols for regularly scheduled inter- and intra- departmental corporate interface. During these structured meetings, all team members present should participate in goal setting and planning as well as in the development of strategies and tactics for goal achievement. The strategic planning system also includes the development of a 5-year business plan for the organization which is updated annually. This 5-year business plan may contain elements of marketing; but it is primarily focused on the financial elements necessary for business growth and performance-to-goals criteria that are required for review by management, shareholders and banking interests.

A well-developed strategic planning system encourages collaborative thinking and action and solicits some level of input to developing goals and plans (strategies and tactics) for goal achievement from every team member (employee). Policies can be developed that encourage employees to communicate ideas via appropriate channels to improve performance in all aspects of the business. These suggestions should have a standardized means of submission, as well as a standardized means of evaluation and implementation by the management staff designated to review them. "The devil is in the details" is an old adage that applies to nearly all phases of goal setting and planning. If something is missed in the planning, performance will be impacted and it will show eventually in the achievement of performance-to-goals. The difference between the Point of Focus and Protocol in Goal Setting and Planning discussions is the level of attention paid to details and the micro examination of all aspects of the business.

"A goal without a plan is just a wish."

- Antoine de Saint-Exupéry

HOW

- **Identify the primary areas within the company where you expect growth to occur during each development stage and during each evaluation of the 5-year business plan.**
  Develop a template that can be used to set 5-year business goals for the corporation that include: sales and marketing projections; market share evaluation; jobs to corporate performance ratios [i.e. personnel needed for growth and maintenance of business status quo]; logistics and performance evaluation of every tier of identified responsibility within the organization. Develop overall corporate-wide goals and specific goals for each department.

- **Evaluate the 5-year business plan and goals against key balance sheet ratios to maintain corporate financial strength.**
  Review all plans and goals against the elements of sustained growth which are as follows: stabilization of the company; collaboration within the company [key executive and departmental]; identification and strategy for key desired target areas for growth; sustainable self-reliance as a company, as well as continuous performance improvement measures that reinforce maintaining the strength of key balance sheet ratios.

- **Develop contingency plans that support the ultimate goals outlined in the 5-year business plan.**
  Developing a 5-year business plan for the company provides an overview of what you want to accomplish in that 5-year window of time company-wide. It is more specific to financial growth and stability and is more comprehensive than marketing plans. It is important that within the 5-year business plan, that strategies and tactics are developed for meeting goals, outlining methods for adjusting goals, and for developing communications policies within the company, and external to the company, to facilitate continuous performance improvement in areas which impact financial strength and profitability. While both 5-year business plans and 5-year marketing plans do dovetail in annual meetings, they should be viewed as separate but compatible, entities and each approached in a thorough, in-depth annual review basis. Contingency planning is critical to meeting the 5-year business plan objectives.

- **Develop policies that allow all employees to participate in an appropriate manner with goal-setting and performance-to-goal evaluation criteria.**
  Involving all team members in all departments in the strategic planning is like engaging all spokes of the wheel to keep the momentum going forward. Team members (employees) within all levels of the company can help to maintain its profitability and assist with keeping its mission statement and performance goals focused on achievement. If employees are involved, engaged and given the opportunity, they are an integral component of company strength.

- **Make a commitment to foster a culture of follow-up at all levels of the company.**
  Ongoing critical evaluation of performance-to-goals in all areas of the company is an underlying principle of the success of Points of Focus and Protocols. It is not enough to simply say "we met our goals." Critical evaluation

includes not only appreciating successes but also striving for achievements greater than the original goal and closely monitoring any and all factors which slow performance down or hinder it in any way. Making a commitment company-wide to follow-up with improvement suggestions not only keeps the company running efficiently, but also encourages people to contribute suggestions as they know the suggestions will be acted upon.

Management Action Statement: Goal Setting and Planning

"Managers accountable for each area of responsibility on the organizational chart led goal setting and planning meetings for employees in their areas of responsibility. They developed sales, financial and operational goals with strategies and tactics to achieve those goals.

Executive management reviewed the departmental goals, strategies and tactics for goal achievement and developed a five year plan, the first year of which became the plan for the next business year. Each employee in the company had some opportunity to have input into the goal setting and planning process and to review and comment on the final plan."

-Hoyt H. [Larry] Larison

Protocol 3

Product Development

WHY

Product development programs are essential when committed to continuously working to maintain and improve company product offerings from a performance and profit-contributive standpoint.

A commitment to ongoing product development creates positive internal and external customer relationships by ensuring that the organization offers a competitive, high quality product line to its customer base [external customers], while empowering the sales force, manufacturing and distribution (internal customers) to meet individual and departmental goals. This is especially critical to companies where sales and marketing, distribution, and management teams are rewarded with monetary performance to goal bonuses.

Research and development efforts need to be ongoing to continuously improve the performance and profit-making capability of all products, especially the product groups that deliver the majority of sales and profit dollars. Sales and marketing departments should interface regularly in meetings with research and development and with finance departments to exchange information and discuss goals, ideas and any valid concerns.

Discussions should cover not only an overview of operations related to product development and products currently performing in the market; but periodically an in-depth micro-analysis of all components of the marketing and distribution systems in place and their performance against established standards should be reviewed. The issues raised within these meetings should be documented in the form of minutes and kept available to all involved at some point of accessible reference, such as in a conference room library or in a digital archive.

This regular interface will promote product and services development, and encourage improvements that will consistently deliver products and services to meet the evolving needs of the marketplace, as dictated by competitive demographics and sales and marketing departments.

"If you keep your eye on the profit, you're going to skimp on the product. But if you focus on making really great products, then the profits will follow."

-Steve Jobs

HOW

- **Regularly schedule meetings within and between departments to discuss current product market positions and sales as well as new product or service development.**
  No matter what stage of business you are in, it is never too late to structure inter- and intra- departmental meetings on a regular basis to discuss where key products are in the markets currently, and how best to increase market share in the areas or sectors you serve. During these meetings, strengths and weaknesses, opportunities and competitive emerging trends should be evaluated and strategies discussed for managing marketing threats.

  Conducting a periodic in-depth review of product positioning and performance can also be beneficial as these two areas of emphasis are closely related.

- **The success of new product development and its implementation is very dependent on a strong and positive interface between sales/marketing and research/development business functions.**
  Sales/marketing and research/development departments are separate functions but very closely aligned. A good performance improvement system allows for regularly structured interface between these two entities. Sales/marketing needs to be continually aware of what products are being developed in order to structure the introduction of those products into the current marketplace and position them against competition accordingly.

  Research and development can assist marketing by carefully explaining the performance of the new products and what their features and benefits will be – marketing can then take that information and develop the strategies necessary to position the products as competitive within the targeted markets and plan the introductions; or, in the case of improved products, plan the reintroduction.

- **New product development is most successful when both internal discussions and external discussions are employed: feedback is vital from internal and external customers.**
  Research/development also needs to interface with marketing to get feedback on products that are already in the marketplace and what can be done to improve them or their competitiveness. Through employee and marketing-driven feedback, research and development can also gain insights on possible new niche markets or new products that can be developed that will fit within the existing spectrum of products and services offered by the company. Sales personnel, customer service personnel and others interface with consumers nearly every day. Their observations may contain valuable insights on improvements that can be made to existing products and/or services as well as new directions that could prove profitable.

These communications are vital to the continuous performance improvement process. These communications also need to be structured so that all key personnel involved in these departments have a chance to contribute to overall goals, voice concerns or observations, and recommend improvements and new product directions.

- **Clearly define how communications related to new product development and/or adjustment recommendations to existing products and/or services should be made.**
  Any new directions, new product suggestions or improvements should also be made available to executive management in a defined, appropriate manner so that decisions can be made and the next steps taken.

- **Develop company standards in documenting communications that occur in formal meetings.**
  Minutes of any formal company meeting should be kept and reviewed prior to the start of each meeting. Minutes should also be accessible in a file or binder or in a digital library to anyone in company departments to review at any time prior to the next meeting. Minutes can also be distributed prior to each meeting so that all attendees have a chance to review what happened at the last meeting and what the review process of the current meeting will be.

- **Continuous performance improvement is crucial in the area of existing products and new product introductions and development.**
  Follow-up is a word that should be integrated into every action and forward-thinking protocol. There can never be enough follow-up by everyone involved when it comes to keeping current product lines competitive, setting new corporate standards for excellence and/or for new product lines being developed and introduced.

- **In the development of the company's marketing plan, which is a separate entity than the 5-year business plan, there may be a projection for the introduction of a new product or products based on the company's goals and current market share as well as financial health.**
  When these plans are developed with management, it is important to include executives from the sales and marketing teams as well as the production and finance teams. It enables and encourages all critical departments to be part of the planning process.

- **New product development requires an assessment of the company's vital areas of focus relative to maintaining financial strength, as described in Point of Focus 4.**
  New product development should also be reviewed against the company's 5-year business plan. It is not enough to simply identify and develop new products, or to assess quality, quantity and logistics issues: it is necessary to also evaluate the entire new product development process relative to the company's cash-on-hand during the process.

  Therefore, a financial executive should be involved in any meetings where new product development is being discussed or implemented. The impact of product development on cash flow, short and long term, is important in managing company growth.

Management Action Statement: Product Development

"Through a system of regularly scheduled meetings, research and development, sales and marketing, and executive management staff interfaced to initiate product development projects that were designed to: meet or exceed the product offering of major competitors, incorporate the latest and best materials available to optimize product economic and application performance, and meet the specific needs of customers as identified by the sales department."

-Hoyt H. [Larry] Larison

Protocol 4

Communications

_____

WHY

Effective communication is essential for the organization to develop common goals and to track the success of implementation and achievement of those goals. Protocols are developed to ensure that inter- and intra- departmental dialogue happens in regularly scheduled meetings to review progress on goals and to discuss issues central to the overall success of inter- and intra- departmental functions.

Rule 1 of ongoing success: NEVER ASSUME. Communication is critical to your internal customers [employees and management teams] as well as external customers [communities served, customers, suppliers, etc.] Departments need to function independently to reach goals: they also need to maintain clear avenues of communication to allow them to develop and achieve corporate-defined common goals and to track the success of the implementation of those goals.

In addition, companies need to develop pathways of acceptable communication and clearly define these entities: the evolution of mass media, cell phones, internet, etc. has opened the door to greater potential for misunderstandings or lack of a "cohesive front" to employees as well as to the community served. Communication protocols are a key element of performance improvement because they stress: clarity of message, consistency of message, and cohesive action.

With the Columbia Management System of Points of Focus and Protocols, operational procedures are developed to ensure that inter- and intra-departmental dialogue happens in regularly scheduled meetings to review progress on goals and to discuss issues central to the success of inter- and intra-departmental functions.

In addition to the meetings, companies utilizing Columbia Management System are encouraged to develop and refine the specific actions necessary to maintain optimum communication channels in all aspects of the business including the communications policies which occur outside of the company's daily internal interactions to external customers. Consistency in communication protocols, both internal and external to the business, reinforces the mission statement by presenting a unified front in all aspects of doing business.

Meetings, regularly scheduled, are one key factor in maintaining open productive dialogue within and between departments and the importance of regularly scheduled meetings, with detailed agendas, cannot be understated. Each meeting should have a standard agenda that includes the opportunity for new business or open forum discussions. Minutes should be kept for each meeting to identify projects adopted, persons responsible for those projects, and estimated timelines for completion. Each scheduled meeting should open with a review of minutes of the previous meeting to track progress on committed projects. Each preparation of minutes should include details of the open forum discussions that are relevant, or agreed upon.

Regularly scheduled and documented meetings, with meeting notes available to all participants for any-time review, keep all employees informed of progress and areas that still need additional attention.

Communications protocols also involve internal policies that allow employees to express opinions and suggestions through appropriate means and channels independent of scheduled meetings and companies should offer clearly defined policies for consistent communications with outside customers, vendors, suppliers, and the communities served. Communication pathways within a company and external to the company should be closely evaluated and monitored to ensure that performance standards are met and that the company perception to the internal and external customer is consistent in conveying company-wide values, commitment to quality and integrity of the business. Communication lines established within the company outside of meetings keep employees engaged with the company's directions and empower stronger interactions with external customers.

Communications external to the company should be flexible enough to address a wide variety of public interactions relative to the course of doing business while at the same time defining those situations that may require review by management, legal teams or boards. Public relations departments often handle these types of situations in larger companies. In smaller companies, it is still equally as important to set aside some sort of protocol so that communications are consistent with suppliers, customers, regulatory personnel, community event leaders, etc. so that any situation that arises can be handled in an appropriate and professional manner.

"Communication – the human connection – is the key to personal and career success."

– Paul J. Meyer

HOW
Internal Communications & Meetings

- Schedule regular departmental meetings and interdepartmental meetings.

- Management staff meetings should utilize department performance-to-goals and corporate-wide performance-to-goal status reports.

- Open dialogue with all levels of employees should be company policy and appropriate individual and independent means of communicating suggestions, concerns and improvements should be developed.

- A corporate policy manual should be developed that covers all departments and interfaces so that policies and procedures are consistent and clear to all levels of employees.

- Record keeping of inter-department and intra-department meetings and a central location for these minutes should be implemented so that they are readily accessible for review by employees.

- Feedback systems, including satisfaction surveys that allow employees and customers to contribute appropriately to corporate directions, should be in place in all departments.

- A policy of respect and open communication that fosters and promotes the generation of ideas by all employees is at the core of successful businesses.

- Communication policies should be clearly stated and refined to address internal and external customer needs, public relations activities, grievance resolution, and corporate image reinforcement.

- Criteria for email communication internal and external to the company should be in place as well as formal guidelines for all communications related either directly or indirectly to the company that occur in any kind of social media.

External Communications

- Criteria for communications at all levels of external communications should be in place to help guide employees who interface with various customer groups, communities, vendors, and other professionals doing business with the company.

- Anything that is put into print that is related to company business should be reviewed by executive management, marketing and/or legal for consistency of the message and for its potential perception by the external customer.

- Guidelines for the handling of proprietary information should be part of employee training and clearly defined for all employees including what constitutes proprietary information. Guidelines should also include steps to follow should an issue of communication arise that seems unclear (who, what, when, where, etc.)

- Realistic guidelines should be set for employees who need to respond to email inquiries, phone inquiries and other sources of public inquiry. Record keeping of such inquiries should be part of this communication protocol.

Management Action Statement: Communications

"Through a series of regularly scheduled meetings, all major departments on the organizational chart met separately and in interface with one another to discuss all management issues relevant to the company and to decide how to best address those issues through assigned projects and a process of review for those projects until the projects were completed. The ultimate goal of the corporate communication system was to enable the company to achieve and sustain an environment of continuous performance improvement and engage all employees in the process."

-Hoyt H. [Larry] Larison

Protocol 5

Customer-Driven Market Analysis/Market Strategy

WHY

Understanding the customer and the marketplace of the organization is essential to the primary goal of serving the customer successfully.

Protocols should be developed to train teams and/or individuals to: analyze marketplace and customers/ constituents, design and implement goals, strategies and tactics to attack the market(s) and increase market share and customer/constituent satisfaction. Protocols related to market analysis/market strategy support other Protocols for setting goals, for new product development and for communications. Each protocol of the continuous performance improvement business strategy is designed to build on the other protocols to keep the company performing to its maximum potential.

There are multi-layers to marketing programs. Marketing's function is to take the specifications of product development from the research and development team and translate that information into product positioning strategies that encompass consumer benefits as well as product features. It is inherent in marketing not only to understand the company's products, but also the products of the competition and how best to position company products against those of the competition. To achieve success in the consumer arena, marketing departments need to work closely with research and development, finance, manufacturing, warehousing and distribution centers/stores to develop communication protocols with the external consumers.

"The aim of marketing is to know and understand the customer so well the product or service fits and sells itself."

-Peter Drucker

HOW

- **Analysis is work: but analysis is the key to maintaining and expanding market positions.**
  Just as real estate is based on "location-location-location" so is market attack based on "analysis-analysis-analysis". Strategy is dynamic when it comes to marketing products and services: the competitive environment and consumer preferences are continually evolving and changing. To be strong in market share takes a commitment at all levels to serve the customer and the market, to analyze the position of company products and services against competitors, and to develop strategies for keeping products and services performing at the top of their respective markets.

- **In the areas of marketing, new product development, sales and market share analysis, successful companies employ strategies and tactics that maximize their potential for success.**
  Continuous performance improvement is an ongoing process where current strengths and weaknesses are measured against emerging new products or services and competition. It often begins with a broad listing of all areas of sales, marketing, market dynamics and market share in each market. Then it is broken down into all of its components working from broad to finite in detail. Strengths and weaknesses are analyzed against market share and market position in all areas/regions served, starting with the corporate-wide overview, and then progressing to regional and local evaluations.
  Factors such as distribution, warehousing, niche markets,

trends, sales numbers, "boots on the ground", stores and projections for all of the preceding elements are listed and discussed. Observations, evaluations, recommendations are all discussed and then specific strategies and tactics are agreed to, signed off on, and implemented in each area identified. This is the basis for corporate-wide assessments of continuous performance improvement and it should be done annually through scheduled meetings at a minimum.

- **Implement regular discussions with key departments and personnel on competitors' status of products and services as well as trends in consumer preferences and legislation.**
  These analyses are specific to the business or industry your company is aligned with and additionally should consider the emerging consumer or legislative trends that impact business. Evaluation of other competitive presence in your markets locally, regionally, nationally and internationally is also an important aspect of continuous performance improvement. This analysis should be specific to companies, products, or services that are emerging which may cause your company to lose sales or market share. Such threats can be real or perceived. For example, legislative changes that impact your products or markets directly in one regional market are real and need to be addressed in a timely manner. Subtle changes in market share on a national basis due to changing consumer preferences can be less concrete and are more perceived threats, but still may need to be monitored and addressed in order to remain competitive and achieve growth.

- **Continuous performance improvement is an analysis that is employed not only during 5-year business planning but on a daily basis by all departments, including by executives.**
  Each company differs in the types of products and services they offer and the types of markets they serve; but they all share one common denominator – rarely is there a single provider. Continuous performance improvement, consistently

employed throughout the entire company, keeps every employee actively engaged in evaluating not only how to improve their own tasks at hand but also how to contribute in a meaningful way to the growth of the company overall.

Company employees can provide valuable input into trends they observe in the markets based on their interactions with the community at large. Never discount where a vital source of information could come from that could keep you competitive and growing. Sometimes, great insights into market dynamics come from unexpected sources.

- **Schedule regular inter- and intra- departmental meetings and stick with the schedule.**
  Regular meetings within the sales/marketing departments can help managers of these departments assess changes in niche markets, competitor presence, newly emerging threats such as new products or companies, and shifting consumer preferences. These become clear when regular meetings are held with sales professionals to gain their feedback and concerns or suggestions. Marketing can then develop strategies for both short- and long- term approaches, which may or may not include new product introductions or product modifications as well as logistics improvements.

  Regular meetings held among key departments such as sales, marketing, product development, finance, manufacturing, warehousing and distribution centers/stores also serves to provide ongoing market analysis simply as a function of communication between professionals in your company. Sometimes strategies require shipping changes, or warehousing expansions or reformulation of existing products to meet emerging industry trends – not all market attack strategies are new product development. Sometimes, continually improving the performance of existing product manufacturing to market metrics is all that is needed to remain competitive in a given market.

- **Market share is the percentage of the market captured by your products and services, sales numbers are actual products sold.**
  The analysis techniques used for percentage of market share are important to be reviewed annually as are the actual numbers of products sold in any given market. Sales numbers of products do not always equate to market share. Evaluate percentages of share as well as actual sales numbers for each product that you sell and for each service that you offer. Most industry associations in the US, and some government agencies, track and report useful market share information for business sectors and can be valuable resources.

- **Market Analysis/Market Strategy is a Protocol that encompasses market share concepts integrated into a comprehensive plan to complement the 5-year business plan.**
  When a marketing plan is developed, the goal [within whatever year range is specified by the company] should be to expand the market share in specific regions by a specific amount. Each planned market share increase should be attainable. Strategies are then developed through sales, marketing, warehousing, finance and manufacturing, to meet those market share goals. If the business is service oriented, the concepts are the same: evaluate the regions or areas served, the current position in terms of how much of the market share has been captured against company goals, and then devise a plan on how to increase that share of the market within the plan's projection. Plans are reviewed and analyzed against the goal at least annually and the goal is not an end point. As the years pass, the goals are adjusted out accordingly so that the company continually moves forward.

It is recommended that a standardized format for the company marketing plan be developed and adhered to over the years so that consistency in approach can be maintained. These will fluctuate in duration or how involved they are in any given year but the format should be one that is specific to the company and utilized on a yearly basis to be consistent. This plan also becomes the budgetary guideline that the company follows in order to meet the goals while maintaining its fiscal strength.

Management Action Statement: Customer-Driven Market Analysis/Market Strategy

"By gathering information on competitor strengths and weaknesses, market financial strength and customer potential, the sales and marketing department developed plans to gain maximum market share and profitability in every one of our markets."

-Hoyt H. [Larry] Larison

Protocol 6

Profit and/or Goal Achievement-Driven Incentives

WHY

In a for-profit organization, **profit-driven** incentives should be developed in some form for every employee. In not-for-profit organizations, **goal achievement-driven** incentives should be developed for every employee to ensure that all employees keep their focus on goals achievement.

Tracking and frequent reporting of progress on the incentives metrics is central to the success of incentive-award programs and are a primary component of supporting team and morale building protocols. In for-profit companies, incentives are nearly always profit-driven. These types of incentives are programs connected to sales and marketing teams, stores, and at times, production/manufacturing, customer service or consumer relations departments.

In order to keep incentives in proper perspective, so that the focus is on strategic planning for improved product performance, the metrics assigned to protocols developed internally should include evaluation measures not only of sales numbers or other departmental criteria, but statistical evaluation of how each market is penetrated for share capture and how each product is positioned against competitors. For departments other than sales where incentives are occasionally employed, metrics would include such elements as satisfaction results for departments like customer service and efficiency and quality control for manufacturing. Straight sales numbers do not tell the whole story behind market capture or success. Straight sales numbers also do not fully recognize the individual and collective roles of the team that support the capture of those sales.

A good incentive program provides well delineated checks and balances and tools of assessment that reflect the true underlying efforts of each sales territory and each target/niche market, regardless of size.

Achievement-driven incentives are often found in not-for-profit businesses and while the motivations are different from direct sales bonuses the principles are the same. Metrics for evaluating performance against goals are needed to ensure uniform application of incentive standards. A clear understanding of baseline data and expectations related to performance standards required for incentive awards should be given to each employee whose job criteria includes such elements.

"The deepest desire of the human spirit is to be acknowledged."

-Stephen Covey

HOW

- **An incentive program is best utilized and adapted to a specific company's needs as these are custom in design and are not intended for every business.**
  Surveys abound that show at times, people are motivated by wanting to achieve and receive recognition in ways that are not always monetary – such as opportunities for advancement, increasing levels of responsibility, and training to achieve expertise.

  In many businesses, total corporate profitability will affect bonus and profit sharing plans, but additionally bonuses are often awarded for categories like reaching sales quota, profit center goal achievement, meeting or exceeding production goals in manufacturing, meeting goals in credit and collections and in the information technology department.

  Measurable, achievable goals with monetary rewards and individual and group (department) recognition awards can serve to keep morale high in any organization.

- **Monetary incentives should only be employed where performance goals can be clearly and accurately measured.**

- **In non-profit companies, incentive programs can be effectively implemented.**
  Usually, in non-profit companies, incentives for performance are more closely associated to the mission statement and what is needed to keep the non-profit company viable to reach its mission statement goals: these include aspects such as fund-raising goals and objectives, public awareness campaigns, membership drives, research funding, etc.

Management Action Statement: Profit and/or Goal-Achievement Driven Incentives

"Incentives for goal achievement were developed for all departments in the company and each employee was given the opportunity to participate in financial rewards for goal achievement.

These goals were based on a combination of profit based goals and performance based goals. An example of a performance based goal would be: improving gallons per man hour produced in the organization's manufacturing plants."

-Hoyt H. [Larry] Larison

Protocol 7

Team Member (Employee) Job Description
& Performance Evaluation

WHY

Vital to organizational effectiveness is being sure that each employee understands, by developing thorough and complete job descriptions, what they are responsible and accountable for, and that part of their responsibility and accountability is to help and facilitate all employees and the entire organization in achieving their individual and common organizational goals.

Comprehensive performance evaluations at least annually are essential for all employees, and if an employee is under-performing and notified of what improvements are required, then more frequent evaluations should occur until performance is satisfactory. A company is composed of internal customers: these are your sales force, plant personnel, customer relations staff, accounting, research and development, administrative support staff, etc. Each internal customer, or position, needs support from the company as a whole to effectively do their job.

This concept of employees being internal customers shifts the perception from an employee being someone who works for the company, to someone who by working is also being served by that company. It can help management enact policies which foster improvements within the company so that those who are working internally to support the actions and work of others are recognized on an ongoing basis.

"It's amazing how much you can accomplish when you don't care who gets the credit."

-Harry Truman

HOW

- **Structure a standardized job performance evaluation protocol that is company-wide and followed by all departments.**
  It is up to the individual company how often these occur: in some instances it can be quarterly, such as in the case of new hires or temp-to-hire positions, and in other instances it can be annual or semi-annual. The key is to keep both the format and the time frame consistent.

- **Utilize a standardized means of performance evaluation criterion and maintain copies of these reports in both management and employee files.**
  Standardization of performance evaluations encourages objectivity and a focus on factual data, such as sales numbers against performance expected goals and sales territory expansion in market share. It also serves to focus on skill sets in other positions so that performance is evaluated against the skill set standards specified for each position.

- **Provide each employee an opportunity to give feedback on the evaluation and to rebut or refute any statements that they do not deem as fair or accurate.**
  Rebuttal forms should be available and completed within the same day as the evaluation occurs. Maintaining policies that encourage open communication and respectful situations of "right to disagree" keeps the company from developing "group think" attitudes which ultimately will limit progressive growth.

Rebuttal forms are a means by which employees have the additional opportunity to request skills training or further education or lateral movement within the company. All such forms should be reviewed by the immediate manager as well as a senior manager for the department.

- **Job descriptions should be very detailed for each position in the company and kept in corporate records at a central location where they can be accessed at any time by any employee in the company.**
  These job descriptions include key skill sets associated to the job, professional training or educational requirements, as well as expectations for performed duties and measurement metrics used to evaluate that performance. This empowers all employees to review skill set criterion needed for lateral and vertical movement within the company.

When job performance skill sets and criterion are clearly stated and consistent for the position, under-performance and lateral or vertical movement within the company is easier for the company to address overall. Under-performance can be recognized before it becomes problematic with corrective measures taken to help the employee reach the standards of the position. Similarly, employees can motivate themselves for advancement if they are clear about what each of the positions in the company entails in terms of education, training, skill sets, and performance requirements.

A key aspect of performance evaluations and job descriptions is follow-up. Tracking and evaluating performance through measured metrics of job descriptions, evaluation criteria, and communications, ensures that employees are recognized for their hard work and contributions and for those who are struggling receive the attention and assistance they need to improve and succeed.

- **Each successful company has a clear chain of accountability within its departments and specific to all corporate inter- and intra- departmental interfaces.** A chain of accountability is more specific than job description as it focuses on each individual being responsible for the execution of their assigned duties within specific time frames and budgets. Fostering a corporate culture of accepting responsibility and challenge allows employees the opportunity to grow their positions and be valued members of the team.

- **Consistent performance review, standardized job descriptions, and a culture of accountability are essential to professional respect.** When positions are clearly defined there is less likelihood of crossover responsibilities or "gray areas" where things can fall through the cracks. This is especially important in businesses that offer customer service. The larger the customer base, the more important it is to have responsibilities, accountability, and job descriptions clearly defined.

- **One of the hardest situations managers need to handle is the termination of an employee.** Under these circumstances, having a long, well-documented history of employment, of clearly defined job descriptions, interventions, job evaluations and feedback, and/or response opportunities by employees, helps to make the severance process easier on all involved and preserves dignity throughout the process.

Management Action Statement: Team Member (Employee) Job Description & Performance Evaluation

"Every position in the company had a clearly defined job description that was used in recruiting employees and delivered to the employee when hired. At least annually each employee was given a performance review by their immediate supervisor with an opportunity for the employee to comment on the review. The review documents then became a part of corporate records and were available to any employee on request."

-Hoyt H. [Larry] Larison

Protocol 8

Accountability: Monitoring Goals-Related Performance

WHY

Once goals are established and strategies and tactics are in place to achieve those goals, accountability systems need to be developed specific to managerial function to evaluate individual, departmental and overall corporate performance success ratios against goals-related metrics.

Frequent reporting and review of goal-achievement metrics must be committed to and diligently followed-up on the inter-departmental, intra-departmental and corporate levels. This protocol is differentiated from Protocol 7 as it is concerned with the departmental functions and overall corporate structure relative to meeting 5-year business goals. It is also intended to define specifics of individual and departmental levels of responsibility and accountability.

The Accountability Protocol that empowers the company to identify areas where performance may need enhancement through training and further education; as well as areas where markets may not be fully understood or researched and further concentration of effort can be done.

It also provides management and the company as a whole with a means of measuring results against expected or projected accomplishments or gains to ensure all team members are performing to the best of their ability.

"Accountability breeds response...ability."

-Stephen Covey

HOW

- **This is a management-driven, overview function, whereby departmental standards for performance are reviewed against corporate goals on an ongoing basis to monitor progress in reaching 5-year business plan goals.**
  A reporting system is developed specific to each company where department managers can evaluate for other departments and for upper management, the department's progress as it relates to corporate goals. These reports should be standardized so that all departments are evaluating the same performance metrics and objectives.

- **Accountability is a layering process: it starts at the individual level, progresses to responsibilities for department managers and executives, and rises to the corporate executive level.**
  At each stage, responsibilities and goals are defined and performance is measured against those metrics. Once these evaluations are made, accountability comes into play: accountability is a professional quality that can be fostered in any company when expectations are clearly defined, measured objectively and clearly understood.

The principles underlying Protocol 8 are in taking measures to ensure that accountability is part of the corporate culture and that accountability is empowered by standardized job descriptions, objective performance evaluation methods, and strong follow-up and communications among all employees—all the while using the measurement metrics of a 5-year business plan.

Management Action Statement: Accountability: Monitoring Goals-Related Performance

"The company's system of goal setting and planning leads to the establishment of accountability for goal achievement and in corporate intra- and inter-departmental meetings progress on goals are reviewed and the departments' and individual goal achievement results are reported on, reviewed and assessed. If progress on goal achievement is not satisfactory, strategies and tactics to achieve goals are reviewed and modified appropriately."

-Hoyt H. [Larry] Larison

Protocol 9

Strategic Alliances

WHY

Establishing strategic alliances with other organizations and/or individuals that are very important to the achievement of our goals is essential to achieving continuous performance improvement.

Strategic alliances strengthen the position of the company in communities it serves by aligning itself with other individuals and organizations with which it shares common interests and concerns and where such alliances strengthen the company's ability to achieve its mission statement. These alliances should be based on mutual support, common directions and mutual respect. All employees are capable of contributing to the interface of these alliances: at executive levels, these alliances can be served by participating on boards of directors, special committees, and speaking engagements; at other levels, employees can participate in community-drives, charitable events and recognition events planned for partners, customers and others.

EXAMPLES OF STRATEGIC ALLIANCES ARE:

- Suppliers of essential goods and services that keep the organization running efficiently (vendors, banks, insurance providers, legal and accounting professionals, etc.).

- Elected officials and government agencies that create and enforce regulatory policy that the organization must comply with.

- Associations or businesses with similar interests that join together to promote reasonable legislation and regulatory policies that affect the general well-being of the business community

- Associations that provide networking opportunities for members to exchange ideas on how to improve the way their business is conducted.

Identifying these organizations and/or individuals and developing strategic alliances with them is an ongoing responsibility of management, subject to annual review of how effectively the organization is utilizing each of the strategic alliances to improve performance and achieve goals. Strategic alliances keep employees and the company engaged with the mission statement and with the communities served. It is both a social outlet and a means of extending professional relationships with others who have similar objectives and ideals.

"Alliances and partnerships produce stability when they reflect realities and interests."

-Stephen Kinzer

HOW

- **Identify legislative bodies, regulatory agencies, and organizations that directly impact your business and make the effort to become engaged and involved with these entities.**
  Cultivate relationships on a local, regional, national and international level with professional organizations that are directly tied to, or involved with, your business. Examples can be suppliers, consumers, providers of services, distribution, or manufacturing, depending on the type and extent of your business.

- **Identify community service nonprofit organizations in the regions you serve that are associated to the type of business you run and encourage employee participation in non-profit events.**
Examples of this would be a lawn care business supporting Arbor Day organizations; a cosmetics company supporting breast cancer awareness nonprofit organizations; a pet food or vet med products company supporting animal shelter drives. The purpose is to evaluate which nonprofit organizations are closely tied to your mission statement, and thereby build public relations opportunities that will enhance your company's reputation within the communities it serves.

Management Action Statement: Strategic Alliances

*"Columbia Paint & Coatings worked towards establishing
a relationship with organizations like the American Coatings
Association, (chief legislative and regulatory advocacy organization
for the paint and coatings industry in the US and North America).
We also participated in other coatings industry organizations that
offered opportunities for information exchange on business strategies.*

*Some of these groups were co-operatives that pooled the purchasing
power of a number of regional paint and coatings manufacturers to
competitively purchase color systems and their marketing tools, raw
materials, containers, as well as surface preparation and application
materials and equipment for sale to customers. One of the groups
pooled resources to fund a laboratory which worked for its members
on new raw material evaluations for product profitability and/or
performance improvements.*

*The company also participated in business associations targeting
legislative and regulatory improvements for the business communities
in all the markets we served. We also participated in state and local
Chambers of Commerce in the markets we served and supported a
variety of local, statewide and national charitable organizations.*

*We maintained scholarships in university schools of architecture
in the states we did business in as a way of partnering with the
architectural community who influence the purchase of paints and
coatings through their building specifications. We also frequently
donated paint and painting supplies to charitable groups working
to help the financially disadvantaged as well as those suffering loss
from fire, flood and other natural disasters."*

-Hoyt H. [Larry] Larison

Protocol 10

Team Building

WHY

Establishing inter- and intra-departmental protocols for team building is vital to optimize employee understanding of the viability and achievability of corporate goals and to the very important role each employee plays in establishing and achieving these goals.

Protocols related to building a team environment draw from several of the protocol elements already discussed. It is important for each company to view team building protocols, policies, and activities as a separate entity and primary area of focus in order to foster an environment where team building can occur and all members of each department are recognized and valued for their contributions to the success of the team.

Conceptually, formally recognizing the importance of internal customers, as previously discussed throughout this book, helps build a framework whereby all employees interact as though each is a customer of the company and of all departments. Training employees to view each other as customers as well as peers encourages cooperation, respect for all positions, and working together to achieve a common goal. Internal customer is a powerful perspective to promote respect in the workplace, whether your business is a small company or a large corporation.

"TEAM – Together Everyone Achieves More."

-Anonymous/Unknown

HOW

The primary building blocks for team building are:

- Continually asking employees for ideas and suggestions for ways to improve corporate/departmental/individual employee performances. Systems need to be established that regularly recognize and reward valid suggestions.

- Maintaining an "open book" on corporate performance on an ongoing basis so that every team member understands how the organization is performing in terms of financial strength, profitability and overall goal achievement.

  Providing employees with ongoing training and educational opportunities that facilitate personal growth and improve business skill sets.

- Fostering a culture of respect for others and the right to disagree professionally in an appropriate manner to keep the flow of ideas open and to empower individuals to think and act independently and to contribute on the basis of their skills and knowledge.

- Implement policies of mentoring, where more experienced employees share their knowledge and expertise with newer employees and/or employees about to accept new responsibilities which require additional knowledge and skill sets.

- Maintaining a "disciplined culture, not a culture of discipline," by creating operating protocols (rules of operation) goals, strategies and tactics for goal achievement that all employees have input to and therefore understand, believe in, are committed to, and are rewarded when goals are achieved.

Management Action Statement: Team Building

"Our team building protocol included involving all employees at some level of strategic planning and goal setting. The company was able to let every employee know that they were valued as individuals, and as a contributing team member. They were encouraged to assist the company and their fellow team members to participate in and enjoy the benefits of working together to create a process of continuous performance improvement.

This created an excellent workplace environment that recognized individual and team achievement and which was rewarding and enjoyable to be a part of."

-Hoyt H. [Larry] Larison

AUTHOR'S CLOSING STATEMENT

I served as President and CEO of Columbia Paint and Coatings for 31 years and was also President and/or Chairman of several other successful business entities. When Columbia was very successfully sold, I decided to start a management consulting business that would offer a system for managing any kind of business, to encourage the organization to focus on areas of management that would enable it to achieve a process of continuous performance improvement. I reviewed the way the organizations I helped govern achieved their successes. I then made and revised lists of Points of Focus that would evolve a strong operating philosophy for the organization and strengthen relationships with employees, customers and every entity and community the organization is involved with. Then I made and revised lists of Protocols that would guide the way the business was structured and managed so it would be enabled to constantly review and improve all aspects of the business on an ongoing basis.

That is how the Points of Focus and Protocols in this book evolved. They have been favorably reviewed by a variety of individuals from the business community as well as educators in business schools. Most highly successful businesses in the US and other developed countries with a progressive business climate use management systems that are very similar in structure to the Points of Focus and Protocols set forward in this book.

Points of Focus and Protocols are tools you can employ to maintain your company's financial strength, its diversity of products and services offered in competitive marketplaces, and to maximize your company's potential to achieve its mission statement and continued success. You can refer to these Points of Focus and Protocols as often as you need to during the business life of your company. The Points of Focus and Protocols are meant to be a foundational guide to empower you to reach your business goals. Why strive for continuous performance improvement and accelerating profitable growth?

Because as James Cash Penney, entrepreneur and founder of J.C. Penney once said:

"Growth is never by mere chance; it is the result of forces working together."

-Hoyt H. (Larry) Larison

CITATIONS: QUOTES

Page 15. "Stephen Covey," BrainyQuote.com. Xplore Inc, 2016. 21 September 2016.
http://www.brainyquote.com/quotes/authors/s/stephen_covey_2.html
(Stephen Covey was an American educator, author and businessman who is widely quoted and recognized as a keynote speaker.)

Page 44. "T. Osborne," Former CEO, the Glidden Company, direct quote for this book used with permission.
(Thomas Osborne served as a Director of Columbia Paint & Coatings with Hoyt [Larry] Larison, while Larry was President and CEO of the Company.)

Page 49. "Antoine de Saint-Exupéry," Attributed.
http://www.goodreads.com/quotes/87476-a-goal-without-a-plan-is-just-a-wish
(He was a French journalist, and author who won several of France's highest literary awards as well as the United States Book Award.)

Page 53. "Steve Jobs,"
http://www.goodreads.com/quotes/664366
(Steve Jobs was the co-founder, Chairman and CEO of Apple, Inc. He was an American information technology entrepreneur and distinguished business leader.)

Page 60. "Paul J. Meyer," BrainyQuote.com. Xplore Inc, 2016. 22 September 2016.
http://www.brainyquote.com/quotes/authors/p/paul_j_meyer.html
(Paul J Meyer was the founder of Success Motivation Institute and was dedicated to helping people achieve their full potential. His Company operates in more than 60 countries and in 23 languages.)

Page 65. "Peter Drucker," BrainyQuote.com. Xplore Inc, 2017. 22 February 2017.
https://www.brainyquote.com/quotes/authors/p/peter_drucker.html
(Peter Drucker is an American Businessman who was respected for his contributions to modern business in the areas of philosophy and practical management.)

Page 71. "Stephen Covey," BrainyQuote.com. Xplore Inc, 2016. 21 September 2016.
http://www.brainyquote.com/quotes/authors/s/stephen_covey_3.html
(Stephen Covey was an American educator, author and businessman who is widely quoted and recognized as a keynote speaker.)

Page 75. "Harry S Truman," BrainyQuote.com. Xplore Inc, 2016. 22 September 2016.
http://www.brainyquote.com/quotes/quotes/h/harrystrum109615.html
(Former 33rd U.S. President and Senator from Missouri]

Page 80. "Stephen Covey," BrainyQuote.com. Xplore Inc, 2016. 22 September 2016.
http://www.brainyquote.com/quotes/quotes/s/stephencov636497.html
(Stephen Covey was an American educator, author and businessman who is widely quoted and recognized as a keynote speaker.)

Page 85. "Stephen Kinzer," BrainyQuote.com. Xplore Inc, 2016. 21 September 2016.
http://www.brainyquote.com/quotes/authors/s/stephen_kinzer.html
(Stephen Kinzer is an American author, academic and journalist with the New York Times.)

Page 88. "Together Everyone Achieves More," Unattributed. Public domain.

Page 93 "James Cash Penney," BrainyQuote.com. Xplore Inc, 2017. 13 March 2017.
https://www.brainyquote.com/quotes/authors/j/james_cash_penney.html
(James Cash Penney was a businessman and entrepreneur who founded J.C. Penney.)